Hues of Happiness

Mahima Kochar

BookLeaf Publishing

India | USA | UK

Presentation by *BookLeaf Publishing*

Web: www.bookleafpub.com

E-mail: info@bookleafpub.com

ISBN: 9789360945886

First edition 2024

This book is dedicated to you!

*You're perfect just the way you are and I'm
proud of you for trying your best in life.*

ACKNOWLEDGEMENT

I'm profoundly grateful to my parents for their unconditional love and unwavering support since the beginning of time. They've made me the kind of person I am today, able to stand strong and confront challenges with optimism. I'm grateful to my brother whose patience knows no bounds when it comes to my antics.

I would like to extend my heartfelt appreciation to my family and close friends for their invaluable contributions, constructive feedback as well as words of encouragement throughout this endeavor. Their generosity, patience and support have been instrumental in making this book a reality.

I'm indebted to all my mentors for shaping my mind in such a way that I can mould myself to any situation that life has to offer. Their expertise, wisdom and belief has instilled me with the confidence to face life head on.

Finally, to the readers who have joined me on this journey, thank you for your curiosity and for keeping an open mind. I hope reading this book brings you as much joy and happiness as writing it has brought me.

Thank you all for being a part of this wonderful and exciting journey.

PREFACE

Life isn't easy for anyone, period. No matter where you're from or how old you get, life will always be the toughest exam for you. What determines a positive result is how you handle the pressure, get back up again and keep going forward. You don't read a book backwards and it's up to you to look the challenge in the eye and say "I'm not backing down!" and keep moving ahead.

Over the years, after crossing paths with some wonderful human beings, I've learnt how to be persistent and stay strong in the face of adversity. After falling and failing repeatedly, I've learnt how to bounce back up with renewed vigor and confidence. Through my experiences I've realized that happiness is a habit and it requires constant effort on your part to make it a reality.

Through my poems I've tried to paint a picture of what brings happiness and what you can do to sustain it. Happiness comes in all shapes and forms, you need to decide what works best for you. Wishing you all the happiness in the world and may you achieve all that your heart desires. I hope you enjoy this journey as much as I enjoyed painting it!

Happy Reading!

Table of Contents

Mindstyle

A mindset that enlightens and empowers
Safeguards when negativity overpowers
Positivity requires thoughtful pursuits
It guides when stuck in a pool of disputes

A quality that takes time to unfold
Once ready it's a precious mine of gold
Dive into the positive ocean and you'll see
From the shackles of life you'll always be free

Focusing on the bright side isn't always easy
Viewing the glass as half full or half empty
Don't dwell on problems just focus on solutions
Practice self-care to overcome pitiful delusions

All ailments have become psychosomatic
A negative thought can be quite problematic
Surround yourself with positive people
Cast good vibes and life will be gleeful

They say every cloud has a silver lining
Stay positive and trust the divine timing
You are what you think and that's a fact
The energy you emit is what you attract!

A Beam of Life

A curve that sets everything straight
A spark that lights up any emotional state
It helps exude confidence and affection
Towards a stronger human connection

Drowning in the sea of anxiety and stress
A change in your glance will help you progress
Falling into an abyss without an escape
A smile will be comforting like a warm embrace

Life is the toughest exam of all
At every stage challenges will befall
It's up to you to make it worthwhile
And it all starts with just a smile

Wear your million dollar smile with pride
It can really uplift the state of your mind
Share it with as many people as you can
Inviting more positivity is part of the plan

A smile a day keeps the worry away
It's a truth of life that's here to stay
With regular practice make it a forte
And remember it's just a twitch away!

Lightness of Being

Something that brings buoyancy in life
A mediator when you are in a strife
Gratitude is the key to contentment
An attitude to resolve resentment

Count your blessings and be grateful
Cherish those who make your life beautiful
Help the needy and make someone smile
Saying thank you is always in style

Release from past regrets and future anxieties
Fulfillment from the present you earn with ease
It teaches you to not take things for granted
You realize you got more than you demanded

What heals and enhances all relations
Can help overcome all your limitations
A thank you can make anyone's day
The mantra is to be grateful everyday

It takes time to make it a practice
And embrace life's every facet
Bringing joy is so easy who knew
It starts with a simple Thank You!

A Partner in Crime

A shoulder to cry
A partner in crime,
Mere words can't define
These friends of mine

You don't need a million
Just a fair few,
That fits your definition
Of a friend who's true

Will never forget those days of school
Hiding each other's books and keeping cool
Playing red hand, till one of us concedes
Turning our pictures, into hysterical memes

They laugh with you, sometimes at you
Re-enact famous scenes, without a cue
We fought for days, then made up too
Whose fault it was, no one knew

Even when we get old and wrinkly
We'll cherish these moments sincerely
Reminiscing with toothless smiles
Reliving those days with tears in our eyes

Sitting on a porch with old pictures in hand
"The time we spent together was always grand"
We sit and complain "where the world is going,
Times were better when we were growing"

So don't forget, to give your friend a call
And make memories for you to recall
Commemorate the days that you did slay
A family you choose is here to stay!

Vortex of Whimsy

It entertains and lightens the mood
With which joy and laughter are renewed
Humor invokes a funny connection
Steering facts into a witty direction

Honey-comb makes the bee's hair sticky
A plateau is the highest form of flattery
An art contest always ends in a draw
Being poker-faced should be against the law

Laughter is the best medicine
It tastes sweeter in comparison
All that giggling can trigger bellyache
Or make you fall off a chair by mistake

Living each day with a punchline
Can make you age like fine wine
A laugh a day keeps the anxiety away
Tears of joy will make everything okay

Comedy is a happy-go-lucky's secret
Taking all troubles with a pinch of wit
Laugh it off till your nose gets runny
What's the point if it's not funny!

The Thought Express

A train that runs on emotions,
And has no destination
An express that operates on,
Each and every contemplation
If you're in the driver's seat,
It's a journey fulfilled
If you're the passenger,
Then you're bound to get grilled

It keeps you up all night,
With its sharp twists and turns
You are an audience to your mind,
Who sits and observes
It's a boon when you're learning,
Or solving a problem too
And can also lead to ailments,
When there's nothing to pursue

The moment you feel,
Like the engine picking up speed
Take a breath, pull the breaks,
And you will certainly be freed
Come back into reality,
And look at the world around you
Forget about those "what ifs",
And your life will seem brand new

A lot needs to be done,
So take it one step at a time
Relax, review and rewire,
For your own peace of mind
Clear your mind of the chatter,
Like the calm ocean blue
Practice mindfulness daily,
And sit for meditation too

Thinking isn't bad,
For it's the very nature of your brain
As long as it's not on autopilot,
You will always be humane
You need to take charge,
To see a world unexplored
To those of you who are ready,
I say "Welcome Aboard!"

The Moral Compass

A path less traveled, devoid of any shortcuts
Once taken, forget about ifs and buts
Bitter at first with a sweet aftertaste
Lessons from the trials you have faced

To differentiate right from wrong
You need to be mentally strong
It's imparted when you're a kid
A reflection of how you've lived

It helps in taking a suitable action
Instead of an impulsive reaction
Your values define who you are
Attained as a medal or a scar

Patience is a virtue and so is staying true
Be kind to everyone and respect will ensue
Modesty keeps your feet on the ground
With compassion, inner peace can be found

Take charge of your life and be its driver
What breaks you makes you wiser
You'll be remembered not as an actor
But a person with a great character

Essence of Life

What gives definition to the mode of living
Assures well being of the body and mind
Good health demands efforts from the willing
A combination of various factors aligned

A lifelong journey of healthy habits
Involves emotional and physical welfare
It can minimize reliance on pricy tablets
Commit to physical activity and self-care

Eat a balanced diet and stay hydrated
Practice mindfulness to manage stress
Any risk of ailments will get mitigated
Take heed of what your body requests

Enjoy a higher quality of life
Treat your body just like a temple
Be cautious as misinformation is rife
Choose a lifestyle that fits and is simple

Good health fosters good relations
Follow your regimen fully, not just partly
Despite the season you'll be in prime condition
Hope this verse finds you hale and hearty!

Piece of Mind

Sensations due to a chemical reaction
Complex outcome of routine interaction
An emotion is the voice of the soul
It may or may not be in your control

Anger, fear, sadness and joy
Make up mind's greatest ploy
Is their deployment in your hands
Or are you enslaved to their demands?

If you're angry then go for a walk
Rid your anxiety by having a talk
If in doubt then write them down
Multiply joy by spreading them around

Express your feelings in their entirety
So as long as it's with sobriety
Don't lock them away in your heart
Once bottled up it's tough to depart

Negative emotions need a healthy outlet
The positive ones should be an asset
For some its expression is quite irrelevant
To them I ask, are you emotionally intelligent?

In the Wake of Sleep

Solace from the day, we seek
Flickering eyes, they seem to speak
Of a search for a cozy sanctuary
Wanting to clear the day's cache memory

Our mind can no longer comprehend
In the hopes, for the day to end
We get on with our night's routine
And with that, we go to sleep

Muscles relax
Thoughts collapse
Hearts beat slow
Is that all we know?

What happens when we fall asleep
Does our brain really go bleak?
We dive into the inner dimension
Dreams they call it, a mind's reflection

An untold story starts to unfold
It's a whole new world, behold!
A past memory you experience anew
Or something unknown, you pursue

You may not remember it clearly
Having lived a different reality
It's a matter of time before you're awake
From an endless world that you did create

A pointless endeavor, you need not share
Or having a creative inspiration, au contraire
It's up to you to decide,
Forget it or let it remind
That you have a potential hidden inside
To be yourself and feel alive

You say you sleep, but do you really?
It's an adventure, so get ready silly
I did my part and now it's time
With a mighty yawn I say goodnight!

Echo of Symphony

A beat that transcends every emotion
It's an expression of the words unspoken
A universal language of the beating heart
Its composition is a work of art

Music speaks louder than words
Heed the essence to which it refers
What seems to be mere noise to our ears
Its sensation is more profound than it appears

Music creates memories; for which it sure has a flair
An echo of emotions about someone or somewhere
Accompanied by nostalgia and a tear or two
It takes us back to that moment, right on cue

A melancholic or a cheerful remembrance
It taps into our feelings in pure defiance
A rhythm that touches the soul of the masses
It sways us in unison as the first chord advances

Music has power, make use of it completely
Feel the beat, sing along and dance it out freely
Decide what does or doesn't get your vibe
You are the conductor in the orchestra of your life

Music that we discover throughout our journey
Shows who we were and who we set out to be
A complex arrangement that sets you free
Music in an emotion; wouldn't you agree?

Expressway

What gives voice to your perceptions
And helps in making human connections
Communication is what binds us all
An exchange of ideas through text or call

It's important to vocalize your views
But be careful of the words you choose
When you speak you need clarity of thought
"How" is more significant than the "What"

In every discussion that you incline towards
Eyes and gestures speak louder than words
When in a dialogue always look for signs
In time you'll learn to read between the lines

Words are more powerful than you may think
Can uplift someone's spirits or make them sink
Listening is always more crucial than talking
Sometimes silence can be more rewarding

Life is way too short to have regrets
Express away before your heart forgets
Point of view is more important than the view
A simple hello can change your life who knew!

The Journey Within

The one person who's always ignored
So many facets that need to be explored
Self-love should be the utmost priority
In life's quest, it gives better clarity

Embrace yourself with all your quirks
It makes you unique, they're your perks
Be kind to yourself when going gets tough
Know your true value like a diamond in rough

Talk to yourself and replace self-criticism
Speak positive affirmations, remove cynicism
Forgive and forget the mistakes of your past
In the story of your life, you choose who to cast

Follow your heart and discover your passion
Relishing the simple joys is always in fashion
Step into nature and feel its power
Practice meditation to reach a level higher

In search of love, those who have traversed
To them I say, learn to love yourself first
You will vibrate at a higher frequency
When you're on a road to self-discovery!

Chasing Time

The one and only unit that measures our existence
A chime or a tick that passes in an instance
The one thing that has been provided equally to all
It's free, yet priceless; how you spend it is your call

One can only wonder at the marvel that is time
It can only be felt after a tick or a chime
Yet we worry about "What Was" & "What Will Be"
As it compels us, to reminisce and foresee

Time can be relative, as the journey of life uncovers
In abundance for some, while in scarcity for others
Like the leaves on a tree or the candles on a cake
We are enslaved to its outcome without an escape

Time heals all wounds, it's a universal remedy
It tells if you're merely existing, or living with sincerity
Don't count your time, instead "make your time count"
Live life like an adventure & your purpose will be found

Time is for everybody; you have to make it your own
Don't chase it, embrace it; it's a skill you've got to hone
Learn from the past, plan for the future, but live today
Make each and every day more memorable than
yesterday!

Taste of Life

A fuel that gets you in motion
Crafted into a perfect potion
Food is the essence of life
Its creator a master of knife

Food awakens all senses
From when its prep commences
A bite down memory lane
Can take you to your roots again

Preparing food is a work of art
It's soulful when prepared with heart
An appetizer, main course or dessert
A wholesome treat like a musical concert

The stomach truly rules the mind
Its power is highly undermined
One should never skip a meal
If overall well being is your deal

Some eat for body while others for soul
So be a foodie but keep control
Certain aromas can make heads turn
With countless cuisines for you to learn

Just a dash of oil and a pinch of salt
That's all it takes to give you food for thought
Bring soul to the recipe to spread glee
Gather your loved ones and say Bon Appétit!

Break Away

When you are at the end of your rope
Taking another step seems out of scope
Don't worry just hit pause and unwind
The body needs rest and so does the mind

Close your eyes and breathe deeply
It's a requisite to improve productivity
Take a walk in the park or sip some coffee
Listen to the needs of your mind and body

Step away from your work and the hustle
You'll find the missing piece of the puzzle
When you look at the world from a distance
You perceive a better view of your existence

Integrate a digital detox or go off the grid
In this bustle how else will your mind rebuild?
Listen to relaxing music or read a book
Take up a new hobby like learning to cook

Whenever you run out of energy
Take a break and you'll be ready
Better equipped to beat the hurdles
It's a break with no commercials!

The Big Picture

Everything happens for a reason
Even nature changes each season
Flowers bloom to wither in fall
Ready no matter what may befall

Sometimes things happen without consent
To fall in place in ways you never dreamt
You may not see the reason at first
Eventually you'll grasp the lessons learnt

When life throws a challenge at you
It's to make you learn a thing or two
Don't get bogged down and be strong
You'll be rerouted to where you belong

You never meet anyone by chance
They all have a role to play in advance
They set the stage for the next chapter
In your life they become a significant factor

Don't blame your stars for your situation
Have faith and you'll find an explanation
Those who think it's just conjecture
All you have to do is see the bigger picture!

Snakes and Ladders

Success begins where the comfort zone ends
You may hit a roadblock or two on the way
Learn from failures and your graph ascends
Challenge your limits every step of the way

Continuous improvement sparks confidence
Celebrate your achievements as it's essential
Boosts motivation and affirms competence
Attests that you're brimming with potential

When you do what couldn't be done
Amidst the doubts that couldn't be unheard
That's when your climb to success begun
You'll triumph over adversity undeterred

Life is a game that needs to be savored
More doors open when the one in front closes
Give your best and your luck will be favored
Make lemonade from lemons that life imposes

What's meant for you will find its way to you
Universe has a funny way of working things out
In life's canvas, perfection is the enemy who knew
Peruse your previous chapters when in doubt!

www.ingramcontent.com/pod-product-compliance
Lightning Source LLC
LaVergne TN
LVHW021349200726

843509LV00014B/2746